JOB SEARCH

5 new strategies guaranteed to help you
get your next job in a career
that is right for you

by

LYMAN ROSE

with
Bryson Walker

Copyright © 2024 by Lyman Rose and Walkercrest

All rights reserved. No part of this book may be used or reproduced in any form whatsoever without written permission except for brief quotations in critical articles or reviews.

Printed in the United States of America.

For more information contact :
publishing@walkercrest.com

Author – Lyman Rose
Editor and contributing author – Bryson Walker
Book design – Bryson Walker

ISBN - Paperback: 9798339014188

First Edition: October 2024

Dedication

This book is dedicated to those who feel temporarily hopeless and depressed due to unemployment.

We who have participated in publishing this book have been in your shoes.

If you are struggling to provide the income you need to survive, it is our sincere desire that this book will give you hope, encouragement, and guide you to prosperity.

CONTENTS

INTRODUCTION

CHAPTER ONE: FIND WHAT YOU WANT TO DO 1

CHAPTER TWO: CREATE A RESUME THAT GETS AN INTERVIEW .. 14

CHAPTER THREE: SOCIAL MEDIA IS CRITICAL 45

CHAPTER FOUR: NETWORKING, TYING IT ALL TOGETHER 52

CHAPTER FIVE: FOCUSING THE INTERVIEW THE RIGHT WAY 65

CONCLUSION 98

Introduction

Being unemployed or underemployed can be extremely difficult and can cause a great deal of anxiety and stress. It can start you thinking that you are worthless and that no one wants you or that you don't have much value.

I was unemployed for 11 months and it was one of the most difficult times of my life. I am the breadwinner in our family and my wife and I have 9 children. Being without a job was frightening and humiliating at the same time.

I joined an employment group and was exposed to several incredibly helpful ideas and suggestions. It is these ideas and thoughts that I have decided to write about. Several of the people who were in the group and shared their thoughts have moved on but their information was so valuable to me that I had to put it on paper as a resource for others who are going through the same difficulty that I was experiencing.

Here's one thing it took me weeks to figure out when I was unemployed: I needed to approach my searching for a job *as if that WERE my full-time job.*

I gave myself a mandate that I would spend as much time searching for a job as I normally would work at a job. I put together a calendar and tracked 8 hours of effort every day. How serious was I? How serious are you? I got up in the morning, showered, got dressed, had a small breakfast and was totally ready by 8:00 AM. Then I kept my nose to the grindstone until at least 5:00 PM with very few distractions except for a one-hour break for lunch.

And I'm not going to sugarcoat it, looking for a job is every bit as hard as working a normal 8 hour a day job!

You may have noticed that I used the word "guarantee" in the subtitle. I sincerely mean it. These are proven strategies and have been successful for everyone in my employment group. If they don't work for you, return the book for a full refund.

Now, please read this book with a good attitude. Apply faith and positive energy. Don't ever slack off or be discouraged. Keep up the good work ethic, and like me, you will see the results.

CHAPTER ONE

FIND WHAT YOU WANT TO DO

AND WHAT YOU ARE CAPABLE OF DOING

Career aptitude tests

There are literally hundreds of online career aptitude tests. Just search "Career Interest Test" or "Job Aptitude Test" and you will find enough to keep you testing for weeks. There are personality tests, skills tests, values tests, interest tests, aptitude tests, temperament tests and more.

Of course you don't want to take all of them, so you need to decide which ones will really help you. A suggestion: don't just take the tests that look fun or interesting, focus instead on the tests that will help you see your strengths and weaknesses. I'll explain more about that in a moment.

There are several tests that are free and others that have a fee. I would suggest looking at the free ones first. (After all you probably don't have a lot of extra cash right now.)

The tests normally don't take a long time so it would be wise to take at least 3 or 4 of them. The more you take, the better you will understand your capabilities and skills.

Here is a short list of the free tests that I took and I expect will be around for some time.

Jobtest.org
Their free test not only helps you identify your skills, but can help you match your personality to the right career field. They offer a wide range of packages that scale in price depending on how much information you want.

Brainmanager.io
They have multiple quizzes that are not only enlightening but entertaining as well.
I took some of the paid tests to get more information. These started at $4.99 and went up. I don't recommend spending too much money on these.

Futurescape.asa.org
They too have free and entertaining tests. These feel like they are designed mostly for students, but you will likely gain some insights about yourself.

jocrf.org
If you want to get more serious I recommend the Johnson O'Connor Research Foundation. They take their science very seriously.

Lastly, for more testing sources you may want to try sites like Indeed.com and Monster.com

There are always more free tests available and employment sites like these will help you find them.

When you get the results back from the tests, don't be too hurried to dismiss them. Of course, if the results suggest that you would be a great astronaut but you suffer from severe claustrophobia, you don't really need to explore that career. On the other hand, if the test suggests that you would be a good mortician, don't just say no. Think about it at least and do some research on the subject.

My sons grew up with a boy who set his sights on becoming a professional baseball player. He came close. But after a career-ending injury he had no real back-up plan. He started part-time work helping out at a funeral home. Now he's a mortician. I was shocked to hear about it and asked him, "Jordan, what made you decide on this career?" His answer was simple, "It fits my personality."

How to Choose a Career

One of the best resources to find out information about careers is from the Bureau Of Labor Statistics. Go to their website: www.bls.gov. You will find hundreds of jobs with an amazing amount of information about each one. They have everything from Aerospace to Zoologist! Just type in the profession and you will instantly have information about such things as median income and degrees needed. You can also learn about the work environment, job outlook, what you would actually be doing in that career field and how to become whatever position looks good to you.

There is so much information that you could easily spend days if not weeks looking at things that interest you. You can quickly see if your chosen field will pay enough for you to survive. You will also see how quickly the area is growing and what the future holds.

Here is an example of a summary for electrical engineers; a career that is traditionally stable and high in pay.

Summary

Quick Facts: Electrical and Electronics Engineers	
2023 Median Pay	$109,010 per year $52.41 per hour
Typical Entry-Level Education	Bachelor's degree
Work Experience in a Related Occupation	None
On-the-job Training	None
Number of Jobs, 2023	299,700
Job Outlook, 2023-33	5% (Faster than average)
Employment Change, 2023-33	15,800

When you go to these summaries, you can click on the question mark icons to learn more details about that entry. For example, clicking on the question mark icon for Job Outlook gives you this description:

> "The projected percent change in employment from 2023 to 2033. The average growth rate for all occupations is 3 percent."

In other words, the U.S. Bureau of Labor Statistics has projected that ALL occupations combined should grow by an AVERAGE of 3%.

But look, as the chart indicates, they predict 5% percent growth for electrical engineers over ten years. Thus, it is likely that electrical engineers are going to remain high in demand.

What about jobs in careers that are shrinking?

When I was growing up everybody started out with a job in the fast food industry. My wife got the typical job for women back then, a secretary. And while I went to college, I worked part-time at a grocery store along with many of my friends who were cashiers.

Well, times have changed. I expressed a very technical, two-word phrase when I looked at the charts for these occupations. "Uh oh!"

Summary

Quick Facts: Food Preparation Workers	
2023 Median Pay	$32,420 per year $15.59 per hour
Typical Entry-Level Education	No formal educational credential
Work Experience in a Related Occupation	None
On-the-job Training	Short-term on-the-job training
Number of Jobs, 2023	931,800
Job Outlook, 2023-33	-5% (Decline)
Employment Change, 2023-33	-44,800

Summary

Quick Facts: Secretaries and Administrative Assistants	
2023 Median Pay	$46,010 per year $22.12 per hour
Typical Entry-Level Education	High school diploma or equivalent
Work Experience in a Related Occupation	See How to Become One
On-the-job Training	See How to Become One
Number of Jobs, 2023	3,399,200
Job Outlook, 2023-33	-10% (Decline)
Employment Change, 2023-33	-332,600

Summary

Quick Facts: Cashiers	
2023 Median Pay	$29,720 per year $14.29 per hour
Typical Entry-Level Education	No formal educational credential
Work Experience in a Related Occupation	None
On-the-job Training	Short-term on-the-job training
Number of Jobs, 2023	3,345,800
Job Outlook, 2023-33	-10% (Decline)
Employment Change, 2023-33	-348,100

As you can see, demand for fast food workers, secretaries and cashiers are all in decline according to these projections.

However, there is one silver lining. Look at the sheer number of jobs. With that many jobs available, there is a good chance that there will be turn over and many "Now Hiring" advertisements for the foreseeable future.

JOB SEARCH

Let's take a look at a position that is growing faster than the weeds in my garden, but for which there are not a large number of jobs... yet.

Summary

Quick Facts: Wind Turbine Technicians	
2023 Median Pay	$61,770 per year $29.70 per hour
Typical Entry-Level Education	Postsecondary nondegree award
Work Experience in a Related Occupation	None
On-the-job Training	Long-term on-the-job training
Number of Jobs, 2023	11,200
Job Outlook, 2023-33	45% (Much faster than average)
Employment Change, 2023-33	5,000

Yep, green energy production is in demand. In a similar vein, here's to solar power!

Summary

Quick Facts: Solar Photovoltaic Installers	
2023 Median Pay	$48,800 per year $23.46 per hour
Typical Entry-Level Education	High school diploma or equivalent
Work Experience in a Related Occupation	None
On-the-job Training	Moderate-term on-the-job training
Number of Jobs, 2023	29,400
Job Outlook, 2023-33	22% (Much faster than average)
Employment Change, 2023-33	6,600

I'll include a few more examples of job summaries at the end of this chapter. Since you are probably eager to learn about a career field that already interests you, I'll just point out a few more things to look for on this great website, then I'll set you loose!

You can look at economic news releases for your specific region and see articles about specific topics. There are dozens of subjects to study and hundreds of reports and graphs to ponder. It is mind boggling how much information is on this site.

Start by simply entering in the job titles that hold your interest, one by one in the search bar. You will find a plethora of information that will give you literally all of the knowledge you need to make a great decision. After you look at one, put a new one in the search bar.

Here we are with Zoologists. This is the header that came up. Each tab will bring up masses of information.

Learn how to use this tool as well as you can. It is a game changer. Now, take a break from reading and spend some time on the bls.gov website. There is much more for you to explore.

What do you naturally love to do?

Go and take the tests and explore each recommended career. But don't overlook the things that you simply like. If you like working with numbers but nothing in accounting shows up on your tests, you still should look into accounting. If you enjoy working with animals but veterinarian does not show up, you still should look into it.

Compare the test results with the things you love and see if there are areas of overlap. Those are the things that you should pursue at least initially. Get all of the information you can and soon you will be on the path to making decisions to move forward.

You can reach out to individuals that are in the potential chosen careers and invite them to lunch. Let them know that you want to find out about the aspects of their job.
Write down some questions so you won't forget to ask them.
These experts will feel complimented that you consider them an expert. Even if they decline lunch, they will probably be happy to discuss their job with you. And who knows, maybe they will have a lead on a potential position. This is great networking, which we will discuss later.

Within a few days to a week, you should be able to determine the top two or three careers that you would love to pursue.
Once you have a good picture of what you want to pursue, the next step becomes easier for you.

As we come to the end of this chapter, let me list a few more examples of occupational outlook summaries. Here is a career field that I thought was oversaturated but apparently is still in demand:

Summary

Quick Facts: Web Developers and Digital Designers	
2023 Median Pay	$92,750 per year $44.59 per hour
Typical Entry-Level Education	Bachelor's degree
Work Experience in a Related Occupation	None
On-the-job Training	None
Number of Jobs, 2023	216,700
Job Outlook, 2023-33	16% (Much faster than average)
Employment Change, 2023-33	34,700

And here are two examples that don't require much education or training but are always in demand:

Summary

Quick Facts: Phlebotomists	
2023 Median Pay	$41,810 per year $20.10 per hour
Typical Entry-Level Education	Postsecondary nondegree award
Work Experience in a Related Occupation	None
On-the-job Training	None
Number of Jobs, 2023	139,400
Job Outlook, 2023-33	8% (Faster than average)
Employment Change, 2023-33	10,800

Summary

Quick Facts: Heavy and Tractor-trailer Truck Drivers	
2023 Median Pay	$54,320 per year $26.12 per hour
Typical Entry-Level Education	Postsecondary nondegree award
Work Experience in a Related Occupation	None
On-the-job Training	Short-term on-the-job training
Number of Jobs, 2023	2,192,300
Job Outlook, 2023-33	4% (As fast as average)
Employment Change, 2023-33	89,300

Lest you criticize me for not thinking out of the box, here are two examples of good-paying, white-collar jobs that were not on my radar:

Summary

Quick Facts: Genetic Counselors	
2023 Median Pay	$95,770 per year $46.05 per hour
Typical Entry-Level Education	Master's degree
Work Experience in a Related Occupation	None
On-the-job Training	None
Number of Jobs, 2023	3,500
Job Outlook, 2023-33	16% (Much faster than average)
Employment Change, 2023-33	600

Summary

Quick Facts: Cartographers and Photogrammetrists	
2023 Median Pay	$76,210 per year $36.64 per hour
Typical Entry-Level Education	Bachelor's degree
Work Experience in a Related Occupation	None
On-the-job Training	None
Number of Jobs, 2023	14,000
Job Outlook, 2023-33	5% (Faster than average)
Employment Change, 2023-33	700

JOB SEARCH

CHAPTER TWO

CREATE A RESUME THAT GETS AN INTERVIEW

Resume writing

Much of what is written in this chapter is from information compiled by Doug Jeppson who shared it with several job seekers on many occasions. He is a former HR manager of a prominent company and is now a much sought-after resume coach. I share these valuable tips with his permission.

In this chapter I will show you several examples of resumes and point out what makes them exceptional.

There are several reasons to write a resume but the most important reason is to get an interview. Your resume needs to convey, in a very brief moment, that you are worthy of an interview, whether in person or online.

What should you do to write something that catches the attention of the reader? To begin with, you should realize that many employers use Artificial Intelligence to search, screen and recommend, before the resume even has a chance of reaching a human reader, so the words in your resume really matter. And speaking of words, the word resume can be spelled with or without the accent marks. Resume (no accents) is recommended for American English readers and résumé for readers who prefer to see the word in the original French.

It is widely thought that your resume has roughly 7 seconds to impress the reader enough for them to look at it further. Just 7 seconds. How much of this chapter can you read in 7 seconds? Adults read roughly 238 words a minute (silent reading). That means that in 7 seconds the average adult will see 23 words. You really need something to pop and get the attention of the resume reader!

Start with Simple Contact Information

Name, phone number, email and website or LinkedIn link. They won't spend any of their 7 seconds there (unless your name is very unusual) but they will know where your contact info is so they won't have to search for it. Here is an example:

Jane Doe, PMP

555-555-5555 • Dallas, TX • myname@gmail.com • www.linkedin.com/jane-doe

COMMUNICATION PROFESSIONAL

Optional Headline
This is a way to state your qualifications and your expected job title right up front. Notice above, "Communication Professional." Other examples might be: "Project Manager," "Financial Advisor" or "Building Maintenance." Look online for some headlines in your career field. A headline sends a

message that you are confident and can do the job. Be careful how you label yourself. This will be the reader's first impression. Of course, you can change the headline to suit different opportunities.

Share your Passion

A great suggestion that came from my employment group was to start the body of your resume with a descriptive, personal statement. This should not be too extensive or too wordy but suggests that you are passionate about the potential job. This is usually called a "Summary Statement" and contains a passion statement. This must coincide with the specific job for which you are applying. (It will be of no benefit to express passion about a sales job if you are applying to be an accountant.)

Author Simon Sinek wrote the book, "Find Your Why." He invites readers to do some soul searching and find their greater purpose. I bring this up because we discussed this in our employment group meetings. If you come up with your "Why," it should guide you to positions that really are a good fit and the help you put passion into your summary statement.

You want to include your strengths and what motivates you. Some decide to make this statement more of a summary of skills, but I got more looks when I made it more about my passion.

Your entire resume must be tailored to the job you are pursuing, and this of course includes your summary statement.

How many different resumes should you prepare?

While I was looking for a job, I had 13 different resumes. Each had a separate focus directed specifically at the job for which I was applying: one for accounting, one for sales, one for property management, one for sales management, etc. You get the picture. Each one has its own summary or passion statement at the very beginning to let the reader know that I am not just sending the same resume out to 50 employers hoping that it sticks with someone.

When readers look at your summary statement they should see how focused you are on the particular opening that they are trying to fill. In my case, my passion statement went one step further and suggested that I felt it was my life's mission to make a difference in that position.

Remember that the main purpose of the summary or passion statement is simply to get them to read more of your resume.

Here is an example of a headline and passion statement:

Budget Analyst

It is my passion to help companies utilize their resources in the most effective way to help accomplish the organization's mission and functions. I have experience in many areas, having owned my own business for many years.

On the next page there is an example of a headline and summary statement:

Experienced Accounting Manager

SUMMARY

Experienced accounting executive with 20+ years of proven leadership. Successful in leading teams in achieving financial goals, preparation of financial statements including consolidations and projections. Well-versed in generally accepted accounting principles. A collaborative leader who empowers team members to maximize their potential.

Put yourself in their shoes

This may be obvious, but you want your passion to align with the resume reader's passion. At the very least, look at the company's mission and vision statements before you write your passion statement.

I have a friend who was seeking a senior management position. He swears he got the interview and the job by including these words in his passion statement: "...to ensure the company generates revenue."

He may be right. What company doesn't want to make money?

Skillfully show your skills

You want the reader, be it a person or AI, to move from your passion or summary statement to the second section of the resume: your skills.

In this section you will highlight the skills you have for the specific opening in order of importance. Remember that your skills don't necessarily need to be work related. If you spent time as a little league coach, or directing a play, or playing in a band you have specific skills from those experiences. As they say, think out of the box and you will find you have many skill sets that you may normally not have associated with work.

Of course, the skills you actually have gained and have honed at work are not to be forgotten. They are highly important.

Start by writing down all of your skills in a list. Don't be shy! Write down everything you can think of. Ask friends and those close to you to tell you what they think your skills are. You may be surprised by the skills you have and don't really notice.

It is important that you don't make up skills you don't really have. If you get the job you will be scrutinized by your ability to perform those skills. At the same time, make sure you are not leaving anything out.

Now, with your list of skills, go to the bls.gov website and look at the job for which you are going to apply. Look at what they do and discover what skills are important to be successful in that field.

As you look at those skills, think to yourself, do I have that skill? If it is on your list, circle it. Go through all of the skills you can find on the website and circle each one that you feel you have.

Next, list the skills in order of importance. If you are unsure of their importance, remember where they were on the website. Which one was first or mentioned the most? If you still have problems determining the order of importance, contact someone in that field that you know or in the business you are applying for and ask for help in putting them in order.

Once they are in order, put them on your resume in either 3 or 4 columns with each column having 4 to 6 skills listed in it. Twelve is a good number of skills but if you don't feel like you have that many, just list them in the columns so they come out as even as possible.

Most people, when reading columns of any data, read the first column from top to bottom and then the next column and do the same so list your skills in order of importance starting with the first column, then the second and so on. Here is an example:

KEY COMPETENCIES

- Problem Solving
- Process Improvement
- Inventory Management
- Information / Data Analysis
- Purchasing
- Coordinating
- Forecasting
- Presentations
- Vendor Relations
- Microsoft Office
- Budget Analysis
- Oral Communications
- Written Communications
- Negotiations

Here is another example, using "pipes" in formatting instead of bullet points:

CORE COMPETENCIES
Accounting - Financial Statements | Consolidations | Excel
Budgets/Projections | Generally Accepted Accounting Principles
Internal Controls | Banking Relationships | Equity Investments
People – Leadership | Decision-making | Coaching and Mentoring
Strong Work Ethic | Effective Communication | Problem-solving

Depending on the job position, you may want to include more technical skills or more people skills; be sure to include some of both.

Remember that a lot of resumes will go through AI scanners

looking for keywords. The words you use in your skills list could prove most beneficial to a search like that and could send your resume through to the next level. Always keep in mind as you write each part of your resume, that AI might be reading it first.

Time to Brag

Once they see that your skills or competencies relate to the specific job, it's time to tell them about some of your **"Career Accomplishments."** This section can also be called "Professional Highlights" but once again, what you list here does not need to be limited to your professional experiences. You can certainly have career accomplishments that are found in other aspects of your life including household achievements and community service.

Remember to focus on things that have to do directly with the job for which you are applying. For example, if you are looking at an opening for a budget analyst, you could use your own experience at home creating your family or personal budget as an accomplishment.

If, through your own budgeting you were able to reduce your eating out expense from $200 a month to $100 a month, you could say that with your budgeting skills you reduced unnecessary spending by 50%.

Try to think of accomplishments that are relatable and somewhat amazing if you can. Look to your professional experience first but don't be afraid to use your personal experiences as well. Break this section into 3 or 4 bullet points.

Here is an example:

SELECTED CAREER ACCOMPLISHMENTS
- Increased annual revenue by 5 million dollars by developing and implementing a new operating room charging system for a local hospital.

- Saved thousands of dollars and 75% of receiving time by developing new procedures to unload trucks in minutes rather than hours.

- Decreased accounts payable and increased credit lines with suppliers by implementing new software.

- Increased sales by 42% over 3 months with creative incentive program.

Large percentages or large dollar amounts will grab attention. Resume coaches often refer to these figures as "metrics."

What if you don't have exact numbers and percentages?

If you don't have exact numbers to quantify your results, guesstimate with terms such as: achieving results greater than___, lesser than ___ waste, …which exceeded expectations, an outcome of over x %, reduced costs by more than x %, resulting in increased productivity, decreased, improved, enriched, surpassed and approximately.

Power statements and the ARM formula

Think of each of those bullet points as a power statement. You want your power statements to be concise and lead the reader to exclaim, "If this person has performed like that, what can he do for me!" They are meant to demonstrate that you have produced measurable results during your career. A good way to express power statements is by using a technique designed by David Mathis called the **"ARM Formula."**

- **A** stands for **Action Verb**. Begin your power statement by using a strong action verb to introduce your accomplishment, i.e., "Enhanced profits" or "Reduced costs."

- **R** represents **Results**. Express the results of your action using **metrics,** i.e., numbers, percentages, units, dollars. Also mention the time frame in which the accomplishment occurred. Example: "Increased division profits 10% from $1.0M to $1.1M in 2019."

- **M** stands for **Means**. Indicate the strength, talent, skill or business technique you employed; by what means did you produce your results. This tells the reader or listener **how** you accomplished the task. Example: "by setting specific goals and regularly measuring progress against these standards."

Power Statement Examples:

- Improved division profits 20% ($4.2 million) in 2018 by implementing clearly stated goals and publishing actual results each week.

- Reduced inventory 44% in 18 months by reengineering our just-in-time (JIT) system.

- Built a $3 Billion nation-leading industry segment loan portfolio within 5 years by application of both target market analysis and highly focused prospecting efforts

If our reader has come this far, there is a good chance for an interview. They will glance through the rest of the resume to see how long you held jobs in the past and what you did at those jobs, but your passion, strengths, skills and accomplishments will have had their impact.

So What Have You Been Up To?

Now is where you present your **"Professional Experience."** This section can also be labelled as: Managerial Experience, Work Experience, Related Professional Experience, Relevant Professional Experience, etc. It is usually best to start with your most recent employment.

Traditionally you would list the name of the company you worked for, your position there, and how long you worked there. This is not a hard, fast rule; the format is optional, but typically that is the information you want to convey in a quick glance.

Acme Refining - Security Guard - 2023-2024

As an older person I found it a little bit difficult to figure out where to draw the line on my professional experience. If I showed a lot of experience the reader might consider my age which could become an issue. Yes, I know, an employer is not supposed to discriminate against a candidate based on their age. However, setting aside the questions about a person's health or cognitive ability, those involved in the hiring process may be looking for someone to keep around for 10 years. (Even though at last report the average number of years an employee stays with a company is only 4.)

This was a dilemma for me. If I were to try to cloud my age by limiting my volume of experience I might miss out on the job opportunity.

If this is an issue for you, one way to deal with this is to not put any dates on your previous employment experience. However, this might have the effect of causing the reader to wonder why such information is missing. Another tactic is to put the number of years at a position you previously held and not go back very far. While this can be effective, remember you are ultimately hoping for an interview and you can only mask your age so much in person.

Regarding a person's age, the opposite is also true. A younger person may have difficulty coming up with enough experience to even merit an interview. If this is an issue for you, it may be best to list the projects you have worked on and provide brand names rather than suggesting you worked for a number of companies.

In some cases, being young will give you advantages in the hiring process. Many companies are looking for new talent, and frankly, an HR director knows that the younger the talent, the more affordable they may be.

For each of your employment experiences, you should show the company name, your position and how long you worked there. If the company is not well known, give a brief summation of the business and what they do.

The Widget Company - Atlanta, Georgia - 7 Years
The leading manufacturer of recycled widgets in North America

If you don't have actual employment experience, do the same with projects.

Here are a few examples:

Clean Up The City Campaign - Summers of 2022, 2023
-New York City Parks and Recreation Department

Writers of the Future - Author of Two Novellas
- Published by Acme Books in 2022 and 2024

Game Convention – 72 hour Game Jam Winner 2022
- Participated as a developer using Dragon Ruby

List your title and your accomplishments based on your responsibilities. Do this for each of the jobs you want to put on your resume. Note that you don't need to list all of your jobs if you don't want to but if there is a date gap, the reader will question what happened. (This is one instance where just listing the number of years will come in handy.)

The following is an example of a general layout:

PROFESSIONAL EXPERIENCE

Global Products, Inc
Manufacturer of green products with world-wide distribution

Assistant Quality Manager   *2023 - Present*
- Managed a team of researchers in the production of green products.
- Ensured compliance with outlined procedures of quality control.
- Inspected and approved all out-going products from department.

Trade Technicians of Tomorrow
An association focused on finding new technology producers

Project Manager   *2 years*
- Received approval and awarded grant that funded research for the project: Carbon Emissions Reducer.
- Submitted results to 11 major manufacturers of gasoline-powered motors and engines.

Be prepared to answer questions about each of your professional endeavors. Remember, the interviewers will want to know how your experience will help their company.

Another section that can follow Professional Experience is **Additional Experience**.

Let's say that you have worked at several companies, but you don't want to make the resume 3 pages long, and you don't want to alert the reader to your advancing age. A good way to include some of your valuable past is to put it in briefly under the heading Additional Experience. Here is an example:

ADDITIONAL EXPERIENCE

ACME AV | Hollywood, CA | AUDIOVISUAL PRODUCER
Produced weekly audio cast for employees telling success stories.
• Camera operation and editing for video production and training classes
• Audiovisual equipment set-up, and conference room maintenance.

New Television Inc | Boston, MA | ASSISTANT MANAGER
Responsible for writing, shooting, scheduling, taping, editing, and directing local commercial advertising and shows. Coordinated station's public service announcement efforts and performed voice-over work.
• Associate producer for City Business News, achieving the highest ratings in station's history.
• Served as station representative on the board of Smith NPA

JD Photos | Salem, MA| SALES ASSOCIATE/PHOTOGRAPHER
Sales of photographic supplies and audiovisual equipment and portrait photographer.
• Became the principal photographer for individual and group portraits.
• Achieved top 50 sales associate status.

Education

The next item to list is your education. If you have little job experience, or you just graduated, you may want to put your education information *before* your professional experience. You decide which would be more impressive to the reader.

List your education from the most recent to the oldest. If you have a master's degree, list it first and then your bachelor's degree and associates. Don't list high school unless you have no advanced education to list.

Certifications

A friend of mine teaches at an academy where they encourage earning college degrees. He personally disagrees with that focus and tells his students, "Get the education and training that is suited for the job you want." Thus, his own sons have several certifications, but did not spend time and money at a university. While he himself has an MBA, his sons are making twice his salary and are very content and well-respected in their careers. My point? Include whatever certifications and training you have, whether or not you have a college education, they may impress the reader as much as a degree.

Here are some examples:

    A&P Certificate, Aircraft Airframe and Powerplant

Or

    Internship: Office of Chief Counsel, Washington D.C.

Or

    Adobe Certified Professional – Adobe Illustrator Certificate

For both college degrees and certificates, list them on the left side. On the right side list the institution where you received them. Like this:

EDUCATION

Master of Business Administration - USA Business University
Bachelor of Science Degree   -   World Trade University
Microsoft Excel Certificate   -   Global Technology Academy
Study Abroad Semester - Brazil - Brasilia Botanical Institute

What Else Do You Like to Do?

If you really want to, you can list other interests and hobbies. There is debate about this section and whether it is needed at all. If you have an interest or hobby that is unique or interesting and doesn't detract from you fitting the job description, you may want to list some items here.

> **HOBBIES and INTERESTS**
> I am an avid reader of books and trade publications on the subject of future technology.

Or

> I play the piano to entertain residents at three Senior Activity Centers every month.

(Notice, I didn't say anything about long walks on the beach.)

How long should your resume be?

Depending on your work experience, your resume can be either one or two pages. It is cleaner to present a single page and it is more convenient to read, but only if you don't crowd it with too much information. Remember, we only have about 7 seconds to impress, we don't want to scare off the reader with something that looks crammed full like a dictionary.

11 point fonts such as Calibri, Helvetica, Times New Roman and Georgia are recommended. Don't use a narrow or creative but difficult to read font.

If your pertinent information will fit on a single page then you will have an easier time sending it and posting it via the Internet.

If your background in the field is extensive and if you have many years of good solid experience that relate to the current opening, you should use 2 pages. Take advantage of the extra space and make it more comfortable to read. But realize that it must be pertinent, well-written and intriguing if you want the reader to spend the time to look at 2 pages.

It is not a good idea to go more than 2 pages. When you have 2 pages it is more desirable to have it on two separate sheets of paper and not the front and back of a single page. If you have 2 pages you want the reader to be sure to see both of them.

Always use the highest quality paper for your printed copies and make sure your electronic copies are in an unchangeable format so they look the way they are intended to look with clear margins and consistent text.

Once you have finished your resume, leave it in view for some people look at it and see if it draws their attention for more than 7 seconds. Then in a more formal manner, ask them if the format is inviting. Back in the day, the format was not expected to rival the cover of a best-selling book. Today however, there are hundreds of different formats that all have an artistic and aesthetic appeal. Again, you are trying to get an interview with the resume reader. The format you choose may be different if you are applying for a position at Wells Fargo from a position at PIXAR.

Spell checking is obvious, but if you do have an English teacher in your circle they will always find something to correct. It's not a bad idea to run your resume through the filters at Grammarly.com. At the time of this publication, they offer a free evaluator. I'm sure there are many other resume evaluators that use AI.

If you did your job correctly your resume should get some compliments. However, you want to accept criticism too. There may be a part of your resume that stands out for the wrong reason. A good test of this is to ask someone to hand back your resume and then ask them, "What stands out?"
Ask people for suggestions on how to make your resume more appealing, but be careful; everyone will have a different point of view. Make sure, in the end, that you yourself are comfortable with the look and feel of your resume.

As you tailor your resumes to each potential job opportunity and start sending them out, it will become apparent fairly soon when you have a good resume or one that needs work.

If you are not getting any offers for an interview, you need to change your resume until it gives you interview opportunities. That is the whole purpose of putting together a resume!

The next pages contain a few examples of standard resumes.

JOB SEARCH

JOHN DOE

801-555-1234 • JohnDoe@gmail.com • https:www.linkedin.com/in/johndoe>

Marketing Managerhttps://www.linkedin.com/in/johndoe/

It is my passion to help companies express their message in identifiable terms to potential customers and create a positive experience so they become customers for life. I am a marketing leader with business and financial acumen having owned my own business and having been a CFO.

KEY COMPETENCIES

- Problem Solver
- Process Development / Improvement
- Written / Oral Communications
- Business Development
- Creativity / Innovation
- Sales Manager / Marketing
- General Accounting
- Customer Service
- Trade Shows
- Microsoft Office
- Program Sales
- Incentive Programs

SELECTED CAREER ACCOMPLISHMENTS

- Have attended dozens of trade shows both as exhibitor and attendee and developed several campaigns that significantly increased booth traffic of attendees.
- Helped to increase annual revenue for a local healthcare facility by several millions of dollars by analyzing billing practices and implementing a new charging strategy for the operating room.
- Implemented a new system for offloading delivery vehicles that saved time, increased efficiency and saved thousands of dollars in delivery charges.
- Decreased A/P and increased credit lines with suppliers by implementing a new software program that accelerated payment of small invoices.
- Organized an incentive program that increased sales by 42% over 3 months by allowing the salesforce to select their own incentive rewards.

PROFESSIONAL EXPERIENCE

Gohealth Insurance
Leader in Medicare advantage, supplement and prescription drug plans throughout the US.

Senior Benefits Consultant　　　　　　　　　　　　　　　　　　　　　　　　　　*2021 - Present*
- Assist Medicare recipients in securing additional benefits to their basic plans by assessing their current situation, examining numerous possibilities and selecting a plan that meets their needs.
- Follow up with customers to insure satisfaction and benefit usage.

Center for Excellence in Higher Education
CEHE was a university with both ground campuses (Steven's Henager College) and an online school.

Admissions Consultant　　　　　　　　　　　　　　　　　　　　　　　　　　　*2015 - 2021*
- Assisted hundreds of students in selecting educational goals based on their experience and desires by determining the best placement for their potential success.
- Helped students through enrollment process by helping with financial aid and other forms.
- Ensured student success by implementing specific POAs for them to follow.
- Monitored each students progress through the process by keeping in consistent contact.
- Kept detailed information on each student in order to be ready to help them at any time.
- Ensured each student feels valued by maintaining a positive relationship.
- Continually met or exceeded monthly KPI goals.
- Maintained Stability and consistency in an environment with an average of 10% turnover each month.

Creative Systems
Owned my own business in the promotional products industry supplying over 500,000 imprint-able products to local businesses.

LYMAN ROSE

Owner   1993 – 2015

For my business
- Managed all aspects of the business including finances, customer service, vendor relations, purchasing, budgeting, strategy and growth.
- Analysis of key indicators, sales, marketing, accounting, and business development.
- Increased sales margins by an average of 15% a year.
- Created a mailing program that achieved a 65% response rate from potential customers.
- Developed a customer acquisition program that brought in 58 new executive level qualified leads in a two week period.

For my customers
- Developed multiple creative campaigns to help businesses achieve their goals - customer retention, employee satisfaction, increasing customer base, etc.
- Captured attention of project managers for a concrete pumping company by developing a clipboard with the concrete pumping company contact info on the clip and a concrete calculator on the board.
- Generated tremendous trade show traffic for a customer by having them hand out a unique flavored lip balm at every entry door with an imprinted invitation to visit the booth and guess the flavor for a chance to win an iPad.
- Overcame the difficulty a customer was having try to set up appointments with top executives by creating a mailing of flashlights with company logo and "I have a bright idea especially for you" and a note asking for an appointment. Over 60% of recipients responded and accepted an appointment.
- Retained clients with white glove customer service.

Executive Association
This is an organization of local businesses for networking and business referrals. It has been in business since the early 1960's.

Executive Director   2007 - 2017
- Managed all finances for the organization.
- Organized weekly meetings and programs.
- Invited high level guest speakers from local government and businesses.
- Set up all off site and non routine gatherings.
- Planned and organized Christmas gatherings each year in various locations.

ADDITIONAL PROFESSIONAL EXPERIENCE

Fort Smith Company
This company was founded in 1962 and was the premier promotional products business in the state.

CFO / Office Manager
- Managed finances and payroll for employees and individual contractors.
- Generated monthly financial statements.
- Created quarterly projections based on trends and previous performance of sales force.
- Set up highly successful incentive programs.
- Installed new financial computer systems.
- Developed bonuses program for outstanding sales professionals.

EDUCATION

Bachelor's of Science Degree - Business Finance   *Awesome University*

OTHER INTERESTS

- Have written several published articles on a variety of topics.
- Volunteered as an instructor for college students in an evening program.

JOB SEARCH

John Smith

(555) 555-5555 www.linkedin.com/in/johndoe/ johndoe@gmail.com

SUMMARY   **Risk Management/Global Operations**

An experienced Senior Program Manager and Market Strategist, skilled in risk analysis, assessment and management in financial and operational functions. A track record of making success process improvements and building strong relationships with teams and stakeholders, able to create initiatives and develop control enhancements. A proven project manager who challenges the status quo and finds innovative ways to be a solutions-driven leader.

SKILLS

- Risk Analysis/Management
- Business Development
- Data Analytics/Metrics
- Microsoft Excel, SharePoint
- Initiative Development
- Project Portfolio Management
- Lead Sourcing/Market Capture
- Customer Engagement

PROFESSIONAL HIGHLIGHTS

- While at Acme Technologies, facilitated strategic business development process that resulted in capture of 3 new markets, including, EW Market with orders over $250M, The Commercial SATCOM market with orders of $50M, and the datalink market with orders of $20M. During 2018 merger, participated in strategy team to perform due diligence and integration for the new organization.

- As a Manager of Strategy, monitored and tracked competitive and market risks to the business unit. After a reorganization at the company, the external risk needed to be expanded to other business units in the organization. Redefined the Competitive Market Analysis function and process to better align risk tracking.

- Working with senior leadership and functional team leaders, identified and validated both risks and opportunities that were underpinning the financial and investing forecasts. Teamed with Business Development and Program Office to enhance control environments by creating strategic plan and tracking system.

LYMAN ROSE

PROFESSIONAL EXPERIENCE

Senior Program Manager   Acme Technologies   Feb 2017- July 2021

Established strategic planning and related functions for the Business segment. Relied upon by the organization leadership for strategy support and implementation. Integrated competitive and market intelligence in the strategy and business capture process

- Led a cross functional team to develop the yearly strategy which impacted revenue expansion by 25% and gross profit by more than $130M from 2017 to 2020.
- Implemented market and competitive intelligence functions.
- Built business cases and performed due diligence and integration.
- Performed vigorous market research and Black Hat Competitive Analysis leading to more robust bids and growing orders by 20% from 2017 to 2020.

Strategy Project Manager   Widget Financial   Dec 2010 – Jan 2017

Trusted with an impactful role based on strong financial, operating, team building, and leadership performance. Relied upon by senior leadership for strategic understanding and market direction.

- Reached a market share of over 80% in core market in 2015 assisted by understanding the different market segments through multi-market segment analysis
- Increased market share and presence in new markets by 5% from 2014 to 2017 by the implementation of strategy and market research process to new business units.
- Entered two new markets with disruptive technologies. Lead a skilled market analysis and product market analysis team to develop strategy, entry points, and market environments

MILITARY SERVICE

Retired Commissioned Officer, Lieutenant Colonel – Field Artillery and Information Operations   1993-2018

EDUCATION AND CERTIFICATION

MBA in Global Management • World School of Strategy, New York, NY
Bachelor of Science Accounting • Science University, Washington, D.C.
United States Top Secret Clearance

JOB SEARCH

John Jones
555-555-5555 | johndoe@yahoo.com | linkedin.com/in/johndoe

DIRECTOR, APPEALS & GRIEVANCES
LARGE PROCESS MANAGEMENT | NEGOTIATION TEAMS

Expert in Appeal Negotiations. Goal-oriented, people-focused, and accomplished leader skilled at directing and leading large projects and teams utilizing strong collaborative abilities. Demonstrated ability to oversee large processes. Proven experience in the development/management of operational and capital budgets.

CORE COMPETENCIES

Appeal Negotiations | CMS Guidelines | Client Relationship Management | Operational Budgets | Strategic Initiatives
Collaboration and Communications | Claims Processing Systems
Strategic Planning | Strategic Initiatives | Regulatory Compliance

PROFESSIONAL EXPERIENCE

MULTIPLAN, Anytown, CO - 1991 - 2023
A healthcare cost management company that provides technology-enabled provider network, negotiation, claim and payment services

Director of Operations
Directed the operations of the Key product line, specializing in appeal negotiations. Responsible for driving business growth and the maintenance of the pricing Data functions and navigating Regulatory Compliance in the industry. Managed the product's operation budget, staffing and activities.

Key Contributions and Accomplishments
- Oversaw appeal negotiation teams that serviced **22,000+ facility claims** per quarter by implementing productivity monitoring and setting aggressive accountability goals.
- Generated $122M in negotiated quarterly Health Care savings, **consistently exceeding or meeting department goals** year by year.
- Oversaw the creation and transition of a second in-house claims processing system by using **strong collaboration and communication skills**.
- Cultivated all client relationships for the Key product.

ADDITIONAL RELEVANT EXPERIENCE

Manager of Negotiation Services
Managed the Negotiation process of the Key product line. Supervised 35 + employees, including the Negotiation Services team and the Negotiation Support team.

Key Contributions and Accomplishments
- Created, set, and directed departmental goals and reports used for team performance.
- Improved metrics performance every year that exceeded budgeted projections.
- Created and implemented a support team to assist in negotiations and provide liaison services to our clients.

Facility Bill Negotiator
Serviced individual claim appeals. Managed a queue of claim appeals, contacting providers, and negotiating on behalf of our clients. Became the top performer on the team.

Key Contributions and Accomplishments
- Created training scripts for the team during the first month of employment.
- Assisted in creation of a patient advocacy mailing process.
- Became the top negotiator within the first year of employment.

EDUCATION
Bachelor of Science (BS) in Business Administration
NEW STATE UNIVERSITY

CERTIFICATIONS
Licensed Health/Work Comp Adjuster -- License IA-946729

COMMUNITY SERVICE
Served in many leadership roles in the local community, overseeing large youth groups, including directing, planning, and leading annual summer camps and group activities.
Currently serving as the HOA President of my local community.

JOB SEARCH

Here is a one-page layout:

Jane Doe

555-555-5555 • janedoe123@gmail.com

Office Assistant

My driving force is to help run the interior of the office efficiently so that the focus of the company can be on the customer and delivering excellent customer service.

Key Competencies

- Excellent Memory
- Microsoft Office
- Effective Communicator
- Process Development
- Critical Thinking and Problem Solving
- Process Improvement

Selected Career Accomplishments

- Increased production of compound hunting and target bows by 300% by organizing my station in a way that had not been practiced and was far more efficient.
- Through the use of different tools, I was able to replace four times as many encoder receiver transmitters as the other technicians on my team.

Professional Experience

Johnson's Archery
World leader in production of target and hunting compound and traditional bows.

Bow Builder   2021-present
- Attached strings to target and hunting compound bows
- Assembled cams and modules for hunting and target bows.
- Assembled target and hunting compound bows by determining the correct parts, order and processes to assemble them in a timely manner.

City Water Department
Municipal water agency for Emerald City   2019-2021

Water Meter Team Member
- Changed water encoder receiver transmitters as needed.
- Changed broken or damaged water meters.
- Changed live water valves with minimal interruption of water flow.
- Changed water main lines in accordance with regular maintenance.
- Installed fire hydrants

EDUCATION

Bachelor's of Science Degree - Business Finance (graduation date 2025)   SLCC

OTHER INTERESTS

I enjoy gardening and am a member of the Amateur Horticulture Society

Spice it up

Although you have to be careful to add just the right amount of spice, depending on the position and the company, put yourself in the shoes of the resume reader. After a few hundred resumes, their job probably begins to get boring and they would appreciate something that breaks up the monotony. Consider using colors to clarify and accent different sections. Look online at different layouts, choose one that suits your personality and the personality of the career field. A job seeker in our employment group found several useful templates on Etsy. Bottom line: Help the reader to VISUALIZE how your qualifications will serve their company.

Now we move on to a document that introduces the resume.

Cover Letters - can they help?

Cover letters are a great tool to help to get your resume read. What is a cover letter? It is a brief notice to the potential employer that you are interested and qualified for the position they are offering. I have just as many different cover letters as I have resumes because each cover letter introduces a specific resume to the potential reader.

Cover letters allow you to engage in storytelling and conversation where a resume is mostly facts. You can say in a cover letter "I saw this position posted online. When I looked into the responsibilities and qualifications, it seemed like a great fit." Or you can talk about the experience that they will see on your resume in a little different light. "I have been involved in business management for many years, honing my skills and exacting my craft."

If the story is compelling enough, they will be eager to look at your resume and hopefully, as a result, grant you an interview.

There are different opinions about the size of a cover letter. Some experts suggest the letter needs to be very brief because of the 7-second rule. Others feel like this is a chance to tell several stories or express many skills in a different format. There are some that believe the cover letter is a total necessity and others that feel like it is totally optional.

Regarding cover letters, my suggestion is simple: if you think the cover letter will:
1. Actually be read,
2. By someone who wants to know a little bit more about your personality,
3. And will persuade or even compel them to want to meet with you,
4. Then write it.

You will have to experiment with it a bit to find out what works the best for you. Again, try it out on your warm market.

I also found that for me, a fairly brief cover letter was the best way to get the attention of the people I really wanted to have read my resume. With a cover letter, I was able to sincerely ask them for a chance to interview. I had to be willing to brag a bit and be straightforward. It may seem a little forceful but I believe that helped me and will help you to stand out from the crowd.

You can get online and see hundreds of templates for cover letters. I suggest typing these keywords into a search engine: sample cover letter for job application. Pick one that suits your personality and your application. It may turn out to be a highly effective tool for you as it was for me. I will share three examples here.

Dear Hiring Manager:

I saw this position posted online. When I looked into the responsibilities and qualifications, it seemed like a great fit.

I have been involved in business management for many years, honing my skills and perfecting my craft.

Having owned my own business, I have developed analytical skills in business management, cash flow management, budgeting, marketing, problem solving, communications, purchasing and customer service.

My academic experience includes a Bachelor's Degree in Business Finance. I have excellent communication skills both written and oral. I have authored five published books.

I am a quick thinker and a problem solver. I served on a national power team of idea creators and assisted dozens of sales professionals with successful programs.

I am a team player and would appreciate an opportunity to talk to you about your marketing manager position.

Regards,

John Doe

Dear Principal Jordan Smith,

I have been passionate about teaching since my high school sophomore English teacher asked me to be her T.A.

After college, I taught for 5 years before I decided to take some time off to be a stay-at-home mom. During my time teaching, I was able to connect with a wide range of students and their diverse levels of abilities. Helping them increase their learning skills and achieve better grades was my favorite thing about teaching.

I believe my experience and my passion for helping students makes me an ideal candidate for the tutoring role at Learning Achievement Academy.

I hope you will give me the opportunity to meet with you and discuss the position further.

Sincerely,

Jane Doe

LYMAN ROSE

Dear Hiring Manager,

I am writing to you to express my strong interest in the CNA position posted on LinkedIn. With my passion for providing excellent care for senior patients I am confident I would be a benefit on your health care team.

Having worked as a CNA for the past six years, I have experience and a deep understanding of both the physical and emotional needs of patients. I am very comfortable with assisting in the daily activities of bathing, dressing, feeding, monitoring vital signs, and in all ways serving the needs of patients. I work well with the nursing staff and my attention to detail has kept those under my care safe and happy.

It has been my sincere desire to establish rapport with patients and their families. I achieve my greatest job satisfaction from creating a positive and supportive environment wherein the patients feel they are important to me personally.

If I sound like a good fit for SunnyShade Senior Apartments, I would appreciate the chance to meet with you.

Sincerely,

Sally Doe

CHAPTER THREE

SOCIAL MEDIA IS CRITICAL

It's a whole new and evolving world out there

Social Media

In our ever-expanding world, social media and online communication in general have taken a firm hold and have a super powerful effect on our lives. Examples are: Facebook, Instagram, X (formally known as Twitter) SnapChat, TikTok, Reddit and LinkedIn.

The information you list on these platforms can make or break you depending on what it is and how it looks. All of these platforms can be used to make contact with potential employers. I personally believe you should start with LinkedIn.

The others can be highly useful when you are trying to find out information about someone else like the person with whom you will be having an interview. But you should start with LinkedIn to give people a way to find out about you.

You have probably heard many share the advice to not post anything online that you would not want your parents to see or that might draw the critical eye of a potential employer.

That is solid advice.

CareerBuilder found that 18% of employers have fired people because of something they posted on social media, and at least 70% of employers screen candidates' profiles before hiring.

Don't lose your chance for employment because of something you post on social media. Treat whatever you are going to post as if it were going to be shouted to everyone on earth because it may be.

LinkedIn

Let's look at the benefits of posting on LinkedIn. They describe themselves by saying "LinkedIn is a business and employment-focused social media platform…"

One of their main focuses is employment, and that is what you are looking for!

Start by setting up your own profile on LinkedIn. Go to the home page linkedin.com and join. It is quite simple to follow the basic steps. When you are contemplating what to put in the various areas of your profile, consider the particular job you are looking for.

Choose a background that is not too busy and has a positive feel to it; something that describes your enthusiasm and commitment. Make sure your personal photo is up to date and reflects how you currently look. If you have changed your hair color, post a new photo. You can also put a banner on your photo that says you are looking for a job.

When it asks for your "Additional name" don't put something there that could be embarrassing or that would detract from who you really are. If this feature is available in your area, carefully choose your "Pronouns" or just leave it alone.

Create a "Headline" that demonstrates your knowledge and experience. Remember that it is only a headline so don't try to do too much with it. Something that gets to the point is what is suggested here. If you want to get some AI suggestions and are a Premium member, go ahead. The headline should sell you, but should not suggest things that are not true. You can use the headline to demonstrate experiences such as...

Award Winning Account Manager | Increasing Sales | Marketing Specialist | Business Development

Don't overburden the reader but do get them curious.

List your current job under "Current Position" and the company you work for. If you are self-employed, list your own company. But if you are self-employed, don't list yourself in every position from CEO to janitor.

Focus on the positions that will demonstrate experience in the type of field in which you are hoping to find your job. You may add other positions that you have held that will help with your job search.

Two of the most valuable places to list your strengths are in the **"About"** section and the **"Experience"** section. I advise you to fill out these sections as if you were expecting an AI scanner to search, find, and recommend you. Make a list of the words you would search for if you were looking for someone just like you. Include those words in these sections.

Under "Education" list the most recent and try to focus again on your objective. Make sure your "Contact Information" is complete and accurate so a potential employer can easily get in touch with you.

In the Licenses and Certifications section, list any pertinent licenses you currently own and certifications you have earned.

LinkedIn Learning has hundreds of amazing learning opportunities that conclude with you receiving a certificate that shows specific skills that you have covered. Each one comes with an actual electronic certificate that you can save and/or print to put on display. There is a cost for these courses so be focused on which ones you choose and make certain that they will accentuate the specific abilities that are in the career for which you are looking.

If you have done any volunteer work, be sure to list it in the Volunteering section. It shows that you are willing to reach out and help if needed. If you helped in a community effort or donated blood, put it down.

Avoid mentioning things that are too political or too religious as that can be off-putting for some people. You can describe something that for you was political or religious in less specific terms. If you took a group of church members on a bible tour, you might say that you arranged travel to a specific destination for a large group of people. Keep it simple.

In the skills section take the time to list several skills but, once again, focus on the skills that coincide with the job you are seeking. Put them first and put as many others as you feel like you need to but don't spread yourself too thin. Most people can't be a master of everything.

Contact friends and associates and ask them if they would feel comfortable giving you a recommendation on LinkedIn. Have them recommend you for the types of things that are in alignment with your potential job. Although it is fine to use family members, it is better if they don't share your last name.

The next section is for Publications. If you have ever been published, put it here. Have you written an article for a magazine or an online publication? Have you written an ebook? Put those things here. Once again, if you have been published writing something that has to do with the job you are seeking, put it first.

In the Interests section you will show who and what you are following that interests you. Be careful here to choose things that will help you in your search and not detract from it. Avoid political or religious references again because you could lose some of your potential audience.

Take this opportunity to show an interest in leaders in your field of choice and companies in the same type of business. Groups, Newsletters and Schools will also show potential browsers what you think and where your focus is.

Finally, if you feel comfortable doing it, create a post. It doesn't have to be long or intellectual. It doesn't have to be written perfectly. Just get your voice out there by writing something positive.

If you can, write something about your journey in finding a job or something about the job that interests you. Write something that is meaningful to you that you are passionate about and that others will potentially read. Try to get someone to write a comment or start a conversation.

There are so many other aspects of this incredible website that it would take volumes to explore each of them. Take time to look around at what is available. It is being enhanced all the time and just gets better and better at helping people to find the employment they are seeking.

Job Search Websites

Where LinkedIn is better defined as a social media platform that leans toward informing people about your professional skills, there are literally dozens of sites that are specifically dedicated to match employers with employees. Some seem to work fairly well and others not so much. Some of the best known currently are Indeed, Monster, ZipRecruiter and Ladders (for higher paying jobs) and FlexJobs (for remote workers).

There are many others that are gaining notoriety and have excellent reputations including - Robert Half, Glassdoor, CareerBuilder, Snagajob, Wellfound, etc.

I had the best success with Indeed and ZipRecruiter. They seemed to hang on to the right information for me and sent me leads for jobs that coincided with my abilities and desires. Did you catch that? Register with these sites and they act like an automatic employment agency, they SEND you leads for jobs. Other sites mentioned were not as particular and sent me just about anything that came up. If you are looking for something that pays 100K+, Ladders has some amazing tools.

All of these sites have a search mechanism to help you find what you are looking for. You can look by compensation, field, geographic area, shift hours or a specific company. Most of them have easy online application processes. All you need is your phone to apply.

It's not as important which one you start with, but it is important that you start. These are awesome tools and, after you get familiar with them, they can be very influential in your quest.

The more you use social media and register on these job search websites, the more likely it is that you won't wear yourself out looking for your next job, but in fact, your next job will find you!

CHAPTER FOUR

NETWORKING

Tying it all together

Getting to know you

A survey asked people how they found their job. 80% responded they found their job from networking—the other 20% are liars. Not really, but networking is an important tool to keep in your "looking for work" bag. On the Internet you will find figures that claim 40% to 85% of jobs are the result of networking. It's really impossible to tell because networking means so many different things. If someone is willing to introduce you to another person who is hiring for a position that interests you, that is most certainly networking. If someone is just willing to indiscriminately hand out your resume to multiple people that he doesn't necessarily know, is that still networking? Well, arguably it is.

Let's just say that any help you can get from someone else to get the job you are looking for is a great advantage. Two of the last 3 jobs I have had came to me through direct networking and the other one came from an indirect referral. Before these jobs, I ran my own company for over 30 years. So, in my current experience, networking has been vital and effective.

A friend of mine found his next job simply because of who he sat by at his son's high school band concert. As if following a script, the fellow concert-goer said to him, "Ya know, if you're looking for a job, Acme Widgets is hiring." OK, I paraphrased a little, but my friend got hired about three weeks later and ran a department for that company for fifteen years.

Happenstance aside, what are some ways that you can network?

You can join networking groups that are specifically designed to expand your base of acquaintances. They may have weekly or monthly meetings where you just spend your time getting to know each other. If you are able to find people in the group who become well connected with the others in the group, you can make a good solid contact that can be of help down the road.

In the city in which I live there are organizations like: The Chamber of Commerce, Kiwanis Club, Lions Club, Rotary Club, a Community Volunteers group, as well as church groups and political groups. Additionally you can go to social calendar sites like Meetup and Eventbrite. These are online directories where you can search for a variety of activities based on your interest and location. Activities range from business networking events to music festivals.

Every time you meet someone new you are networking. In fact, it's almost impossible to engage in small talk with someone and not hear the question "So, what do you do?" Instead of making excuses, that is your opportunity to say something like, "Well, as a matter of fact, I happen to be looking for my next job."

One Saturday, I was simply helping some people move into the neighborhood. There were about 4 of us within earshot when I heard that question come up. "So, what do you do?"

Before the new neighbor could finish unloading the truck the gossip had spread that he was looking for work and I'll bet a dozen amateur neighborhood talent scouts were on the lookout.

It is super likely that just by engaging in conversations you will run across people who have the sympathetic nature to say, "I'll keep you in mind and if something comes up, I'll let you know." And they really mean it. But they can't keep you in mind if they don't know you're looking.

Employment Groups

If you aren't comfortable joining a local networking organization, there are online groups that have similar functions. There are employment groups like the one I joined that have meetings every weekday. A lot of automatic networking takes place when you join such a group. In fact, companies with proactive HR directors would regularly check in on us to learn about the people in our employment group. Plus, when you meet with others who are in the same boat as you, they naturally have your back.

Employment Fairs

There are employment fairs where companies who are looking for employees set up booths so that you can find out more about the company and determine if you want to apply or give them a resume. If your state has a local department of workforce services, you can ask them if a "job fair" is coming up.

Here is a sample advertisement:

Chicago Job Fair
Meet with top hiring companies in Chicago.
Location
The Congress Plaza Hotel & Convention Center
520 South Michigan Avenue Chicago, IL 60605

ABOUT THIS CHICAGO JOB FAIR
Are you looking for a job in the Chicago area? If you are, then you need to register and attend this event. Best Hire Career Fairs has provided the best hiring events in the country for the last five years. What sets us apart from our competition is that we identify what employers are looking for and match them with the best candidates. If you're in the market for a new job or advancing your career, you will want to be at this event. Make sure you arrive early. Doors will open at 11 am, and the event will end at 2 pm.

There is no cost to attend this event if you are a job seeker.

Reach out to your current friends and to your old friends and just let them know that you are looking. In just about any casual conversation you should be comfortable in bringing up the fact that you are looking for your next job or a new career.

Go to your LinkedIn and look for the potential dozens of mutual connections you probably have with your friends. Contact previous co-workers and see if they have any contacts with other companies. Look up the companies that you want to work for on LinkedIn and see if you have a connection with anyone that is working for that company.

If in your previous job you worked with different companies, reach out to the people you worked with and let them know you are looking. They already know some of your skills and hopefully they enjoyed your working relationship.

Those of us that have had previous co-workers that are still in our field of interest, can start by letting them know we too are looking to make a move. There are many, many stories of former co-workers saying, "Good to hear that you're looking Jane, guess what, we've got an opening here at Acme Widgets, fill out an application and I'll recommend you!"

I have another friend who pivoted from running a TV station to teaching media production at an academy just by mentioning something to an instructor that worked there. Almost without realizing it he found himself sitting in front of an administrator who said, "Mrs Hansen told me you've always wanted to teach. She recommends you highly. How would you like to teach here at the academy?" He has taught there for seven years now and will one day receive retirement benefits from the job. The students love him. And he loves the students. Well, some of them.

So what do you say when you are networking? That is a great question. Although it may feel awkward for you to reach out to people when you feel like you are coming from a position of weakness, most people understand that finding new employment is just a part of life. In fact, most professionals are familiar with the term "networking" and you can even start with that. "Hello Bob, (insert small talk). Well, the main reason I'm calling you today is because I'm doing some *networking*..."

Every situation will be a little different but there are certain things that should be part of almost every networking conversation. You want the person you are contacting to know what you are looking for in a career. Be prepared and unafraid to describe exactly what kind of position you are looking for and even an example of the specific type of company.

If you are talking to someone who works for the company you want to work for, ask them what they do for the company. Ask them about the culture, the environment, the things they like the most and what they like the least. Focus on their role and let them know what positions interest you. After making such a description you should follow up with a question like, "Did that explain what I'm looking for?" Or "I hope that gave you a picture of what I'm pursuing, does anything come to mind?"

If you are talking to a potential employer, ask about current openings. Express interest and pass on some quick information about your skills. Ask them how they were able to find a position in the company. Talk to them about ways to get an interview. "Who do you know that might be hiring?"

You should come away from every conversation with a new piece of knowledge that will help you in your search. You should also be asking if the person you are talking to could recommend someone else that might be able to help you.

Keep a notebook or take notes on your phone. Write down the names of the people you have spoken to. If you got contact information from them, reach out and let them know you appreciated the time they spent with you. Down the road, you might have a chance to drop a name or two to someone else you are talking to and you want them to hear only positive things about you.

Set networking goals such as, "I will reach out to ____ people every day (week)." Keep track of your compliance with your goal and don't slack off. Contact at least 25 new people a week. Think of literally everyone you know. Make a list. When you get your brain working like this you are bound to come up with a bigger networking list than you at first imagined.

Work through the list and continue to get referrals from them. You will have more potential contacts than you can possibly follow up on every week. Do follow up with the people that are most likely to be helpful. Life gets busy and they may forget your conversation fairly quickly so you need to keep it top of their mind.

Some of us find networking an enjoyable thing. Some of us aren't so naturally social. I personally am smack dab in the middle. I'm uncomfortable with reaching out, but more comfortable once the conversation gets going.

One important thing to remember for those of us who are stepping outside of our comfort zone, is that you may feel weak on the inside, but you really aren't a charity case.

You must determine in your own mind that you are worthy of finding your next job or new career and you are going to be a valuable asset in your new position. Heck, your next employer will be lucky to have you.

Being positive and exuding self-confidence is so important in networking. Yes, you need to be grateful to those who are willing to help you network, but you should never appear down and out. People will be more motivated by your positive energy than by your negative misfortune.

It is a good idea to have both a printed copy and access to a digital copy of your resume with you when you are networking. Bring the versions that apply best for the networking group. After you have sent your digital resume a few times by email or text, you will get comfortable with this and it will almost become automatic. Business cards are optional depending on your career field.

Another document I didn't use but others have had success with is a **"networking profile."** It is similar to a resume but designed specifically to be handed out to people who can help you network. It reads more like a bio and should include a "headshot" photo of you at the top. Look at some online and prepare one if you think you will have the opportunity to hand them out.

You will impress someone immensely when you have the right answer to, "Have you got a card or a resume?" Can't you just hear your response in your mind's ear? "You darn well better believe I do. And it's a thing of beauty! Here ya go! Take it.

Read it. Be impressed. But above all, please, pass it on!" (Of course, you'll want to articulate those words a little more eloquently.)

Send the people with whom you are networking a very brief email and text that they can send to the influential people you have asked them to talk to. Don't make them try to come up with something to say about you. Give them something that they can easily cut and paste, something that delivers the specific message you want it to deliver.

I'll Give You 30 Seconds

To help with your networking, put together a "me in 30 seconds" personal profile. Some people call it your "elevator speech." It is a brief statement about you and what you are looking for. It is a short and compelling pitch that you can express in the time it takes an elevator to travel a floor or two. You should have it memorized and, if possible, have two or three versions. You may want to have one for each job you are researching.

Your quick speech is to be used in networking when someone inquires, "What kind of job are you looking for?"

Make sure at least one version of your elevator speech is 30 seconds or less, that's the proven magic number. 30 seconds gives enough information to interest someone but not bore them. If you are talking with an employer, 30 seconds should convince them that you would be a benefit to the company. Don't make it sound rushed. And if you can tell your audience is really interested, you can add a little more information and stretch it out to 60 seconds. Like the climactic ending to any good story, try to end with a final goal that aligns with the employer's needs.

Let's break down what the speech should include. You will want to state what you can do and how it will help. You can use statements that begin with words like:

I am an expert in...
I have accomplished...
I know how to...
I can do...
My skills are...
I have experience with...

Express what you can do, have done, and especially how it will benefit an employer. Direct your speech toward what you want to have happen. Ask who you should talk to or if the person would be willing to pass on your resume to a decision maker. Ask the best way to apply. Let them know that you want to pursue a job. Here are two examples of elevator speeches:

My name is _____. I'm passionate about helping people succeed. I'm an Account Management professional with many years of experience. I have excellent communication skills at all levels.

I grew my own company from nothing to be a thriving business for over 20 years by consistently increasing my account base and keeping my clients very happy.

I'm a passionate problem solver and a creative and innovative thinker. Using my abilities, I have helped dozens of companies to capture their most desired potential customers.

I'm looking for opportunities to use my account management skills to help businesses achieve their goals by keeping their current customers more than satisfied and successfully prospecting for additional customers.

Who do you know that I should know?

(This is the speech that I used when introducing myself to a person who turned out to be the general manager of his company and then offered me a position.)

Here's another example:

My name is _____
I recently graduated from the College of Culinary Arts.
I'm working part-time right now as a line chef at Italiano's Fine Dining Restaurant which has given me the experience to become a full-time sous or executive chef.
I have my food handler's permit and all the certifications to allow me to step into any kitchen and immediately begin working.
I thrive in the kitchen environment and feel a sense of accomplishment when the food is prepared at a very high quality and yet efficiently so as to ensure the restaurant turns a profit.
I'm very serious about seeking a full-time position with a restaurant that has a challenging menu and customers with exceptional and demanding tastes.
Do you know someone I could talk to who could use a chef like me to help create the ultimate fine-dining experience?

Interestingly enough, the person with this pitch landed a job as an executive chef at a large, upscale assisted living center. He said he was unexpectedly happy and fulfilled in that setting.

The Informational Interview

There is one more aspect of networking that many people fail to use but it can be quite powerful. The informational interview is exactly what it says it is. You reach out to a company in your field of interest. You contact someone in the department for which you are looking for a job. You then ask that person if they would be willing to talk to you for about 10 minutes for an informational interview. It can take place over the phone, in a zoom meeting or at lunch.

You will find that many people like to talk about their job because they are very good at it. There will be some that simply turn you down, but that is okay. You probably wouldn't have a good interview with them anyway. Just know that there will be those that respond positively. Start by thanking them and a few words of light conversation so you both feel comfortable. Reassure them that you will keep the interview to 10 minutes because you know time is valuable.

Have a specific set of questions prepared for the interview. Here are some examples:

"What makes someone valuable in your field?"
"What skills are in demand?"
"What does the future look like?"

Don't go over the promised time unless the person you contacted wants to continue. Ask your questions and listen carefully to their answers. You are not only finding out more about the company, you are developing a networking contact that can prove invaluable in the future.

As you ask questions, it will spark a conversation. You can let the person know that you are hoping to find a position at the company and you are grateful to get a feel for what it would be like to work there. If they ask you some questions, answer them thoughtfully and make sure they feel like you have not just robbed them of 10 minutes of their day for nothing.

Networking is the most essential aspect of getting a job and developing your career. The resumes and interviews normally come after a networking contact has set you up with one of their contacts. I know that reaching out sounds difficult to some and impossible to others, but the rewards will be well worth it. Just set your goals, keep track as if you are simply following a checklist and focus.

Believe in the process. That's what it is, a process. Soon you will find yourself getting invited to have interviews. And remember, it really is all about getting the interviews. That is how you will get the job that you desire.

CHAPTER FIVE

THE INTERVIEW

Focusing it the right way

It's just a conversation

Now that you have decided what you want to do, written an outstanding resume, focused your online LinkedIn presence and made several contacts, you should be getting some invitations to have an interview.

That is what all of the rest of the hard work has been leading up to - The Interview.

For some, the interview is frightening, daunting and causes severe heartburn. For others, it is a routine brief encounter that ends with a "we'll be in contact with you soon" as they are ushered to the door.

In reality, the interview is just a conversation between individuals that are both trying to determine the same thing: Is this potential position a good fit for you, the candidate. It should be no more frightening than talking to a new friend.

Sometimes it helps to understand that you are interviewing them just as much as they are interviewing you. If you don't like what you are hearing, you will, in effect, show them the door by leaving without a desire to hear from them again.

Don't feel like the persons interviewing you are superior to you. There are definitely things that you can do that none of them can and there are things that they can do that you can't.

You are just trying to explore the notion of the two sides working together for the betterment of the organization.

That being said, this is not something about which you should be nonchalant or apathetic. But, it is also not the end of the world if things don't seem to work out. Sometimes a good fit takes time to find and a perfect fit, even longer.

Preparing for an interview

The day comes when you get noticed. Someone has seen your resume or your listing on LinkedIn or has heard of you from an associate and decides to contact you for an interview. Congratulations, but please realize that your work has just begun. There is a lot to do in preparation for the event. As a matter of fact, you will potentially spend a few days, if not more, in preparation.

We have talked briefly about social media and how potential employers can look at your listings in order to find out more about you. Well, that works both ways.

Look up everything you can about the company. Look at their year-end reports. See what types of things they are doing in their industry. Check out their stock (if they have stock) and see how the market is reacting. Has the price of their stock been rising or falling?

Look at the different divisions and consider which one you might want to be your focus. Look at their history. What is their product focus, or as is said, what is their secret sauce?

Find and learn the company mission statement, vision statement and slogan. How long have they been in business? What has caused their growth? Have they had a recent change in the C level positions? Where is the home office? How many branches are there? Etc., Etc., Etc. Get to know everything you can about the company!

Next, if you can, find out the names of those who will be interviewing you and begin learning about them. You will want to look on all social media platforms and find out as much as you can about these individuals. Find out what their hobbies are and who their favorite sports teams are. Find out what kind of foods they like and if they like to travel. Find out if they have families and what they like to read. Find out everything you can about them and make careful notes.

Why do all this? For one thing, it's good to know what you have in common with them. Maybe you both like to golf or play pickle ball. Maybe you have the same favorite college football team. Maybe you read the same kind of books or like to travel to the same spots.

Maybe you have the same number of children or you both regularly give blood. It really doesn't matter specifically what it is but find as many things in common as you can. These will be conversation starters to get things moving smoothly just before the interview.

You may also be able to avoid putting your foot in your mouth.

Here's an example of the ultimate faux pas. Imagine you see a USC football jersey signed and framed behind the desk of the man giving the interview. You say something to break the ice like, "Go Trojans!"

The man says to you, "Oh, are you a fan of SC football?"

"I sure am."

Let's say another person in the room, an administrative assistant says, "How did you like that 2010 football season?"

"Oh yeah, that was one good team."

Then the interviewer and the administrative assistant look at each other with an awkward smile. You know you just stepped in something bad. Using your vast powers of deduction you say, "Wait a minute, were YOU on that team?"

And the administrative assistant says, "He was the quarterback."

Sound ridiculous? That's exactly what happened to a former business partner of mine; different university, but otherwise the same story. If anything, it was worse. Not only did he blow it, he wasn't even given the chance to save face by apologizing. Needless to say, the interviewer never said the words, "we'll be in touch." No, the one-time quarterback didn't laugh it off; he stood up, rolled his eyes and walked out of the room.

The administrative assistant said, "He's funny about people that don't remember him. So, I guess this interview is over." That's the kind of painful lesson you only have to learn once.

Here's another quick example of how to show up ill prepared. One time I was waiting in the lobby with a couple of other candidates. A man's name was called and he walked into the interview room. You may not believe this, but I actually heard the candidate lead off with the following small talk before the doors closed, "This is an amazing place you've got here, what is it that you do, exactly?"

"What is it that you do?" Ouch! One thing they don't do is hire fools.

Review your notes over and over again so you know exactly which person shares which commonality with you.

If there is going to be more than one person on the other side of the table, make sure you know which one is the most likely to make the hiring decision and which one is the boss. It could be the same person but it might not be.

Your focus will be on the boss and whoever is going to do the hiring. At the same time however, try to make excellent contact with the others in the room. After you leave they will all share their impressions of you.

Tell a Story

Now that you have notes on the company and the individuals, it's time to prepare several stories about yourself. You will need to commit these to absolute memory and have them at the ready every moment of the interview.

These stories will have similar parts but each one will show a different strength or trait that you are magnifying by the use of the story.

The STAR Formula

Each story you prepare should have a Situation, Task, Action and Result. This is the STAR formula. You should think of as many STAR stories as you can from your work experience or any other situation that fits the mold.

It helps to put these on an Excel sheet or a lined piece of paper. Practice telling some of these out loud, or even better, to your warm circle of influence.

It may feel like you are stepping out of your comfort zone to rehearse these as if you are an actor getting ready to take the stage, but the members of our employment group were tasked to develop STAR stories every week.

A surprise outcome from preparing these stories is that you actually become more confident in who you are and why any company would be fortunate to hire you. Here is an Excel chart with some examples:

JOB SEARCH

Situation	Task	Action	Result	Title
Hospital losing revenue in the operating room because the charging nurse was having difficulty knowing what items were used during a surgery.	Needed to be able to document all items used in each surgery without compromising the safety of the patient.	Developed a system that prepared a cart for every surgery containing everything the surgeon needed to complete the surgery. Emergency items were still in the surgery room but everything else was removed.	The charging nurse was able to simply look at the cart and easily see what had been used and charge the patient accordingly. This increased revenue for the hospital by 5 million dollars the first year.	Hospital surgery Creativity Problem Solving
Unloading trucks was tedious and time consuming. As trucks were in the dock, the boxes were removed one by one and given to someone in receiving to put on a hand truck and deliver to the correct department. Sending the boxes one by one took a long time and the truck was charging the store for the time in the unloading bay.	Needed to find a way to decrease the unloading time and increase efficiency in getting the products to the various departments.	Used tape to designate specific departments on the receiving floor. There were 6 departments. We unloaded the trucks by putting the packages on the floor of the receiving bay dividing them for each department using the tape on the floor. Then each handcart could transport 5 or 6 boxes at a time to the various departments.	We were able to unload the entire truck in 20 minutes instead of 2 to 3 hours. We were also able to deliver the packages to their departments 5 times as quickly as before when only delivering one package at at time. The store saved thousands of dollars in costs by having the trucks in the bay for a much shorter time period.	Mervyns Creativity Problem Solving Taking Charge
Local opening of a new health care facility	Wanted to have the local neighbors visit the open house.	Created a spacial lip balm with a specific flavor to be sent out to the 500 nearby residence with a note to come to the facility on the day of the open house and guess the flavor of the clip balm in order to have a chance to win an IPAD.	The results were overwhelming and the open house was a huge success with hundreds of participants.	Health center Creative Ideas
Pump company had a new pump that could pump fliquid through a 4" interior diameter pipe. The competitor's 4" pump was an exterior diameter.	Needed to be able to show at a trade show that their pump would handle more volume.	Developed a 4" ion diameter ball with their logo on it. The ball was given out at their booth and the recipients were encouraged to go to the competitors booth and see if the ball fit in their new pump. Of course it did not.	The competitor had a huge number of ball recipients go to their booth and acknowledge that the ball would not fit in their pump. They eventually asked our client to stop sending people to their booth.	Specialty Pump Trade Shows Creative Ideas Problem Solving
A Company wants to get the attention of several high level executives who would simply not talk to them or respond to their correspondence.	Needed to find a way to get in the door of the high level executives.	Developed a mailing that included a very nice flashlight imprinted with the company logo and the phrase "I have a bright idea for you". There was a note requesting just 5 minutes of the executives time.	Over 60% of the recipients allowed the company to have an appointment and welcomed the company representative when they came.	Flashlight or Thermos mailing Creativity Problem Solving Mailing for customer

Notice the Situation, the Task, the Action and the Result. I added a column to remind me what trait or ability each story emphasized. I also added a column at the end to simply remember the story. Once I had the story down and the best way to tell it, I simply needed to tie the title to it to remind me of the entire story. I also memorized which trait it demonstrated. Note that each story is brief but brings out a specific characteristic. You don't want to tell a 5-minute story. It needs to be as brief as possible and still get the point across.

You should have at least one story for the basic things that are part of the job for which you are interviewing; things like integrity, leadership, team player, diligence, problem solving. These are all things that almost every position will need. I have stories for all of those but have shared just a few here.

Just make sure that you have several stories for all of the basics and some additional situations in your quiver before you schedule an interview.

I haven't a thing to wear

Now we haven't spent any time on dressing for an interview. Maybe we should have spent a chapter on that. But, the norms here seem to be in flux. When I was first looking for a job several decades ago, we were told to wear a suit and a tie to interview no matter what the job. If you were looking for a mechanic position, you wore a suit. If you were looking for a gym teacher position, you wore a suit. If you were looking for a management position, you wore a suit. It really didn't matter what the position was, the dress code was the same.

Now I've noticed that the younger the administration, the more relaxed the culture. You have to do your own due diligence here to see what dress is appropriate for the company culture.

I will say however, that if you are going to either under dress or over dress, over dress. You will rarely give offense if you dress up for a job interview when business casual would have sufficed.

The only time I have ever heard of someone getting called out for overdressing was when a friend of mine met up with a Hollywood director. Looking back on it, he says he should have known better. When he was fresh out of college, he learned that a movie production company was in town and hiring some crewmembers. As another networking example, a friend of his was doing some work for the director and mentioned that my friend had a particular set of skills that would come in handy. Soon my friend showed up for an interview wearing a tie. The first thing the director said was, "Oh Geez Louise, get rid of that tie!"

Fortunately, my friend had the right response. "Gladly."

"Ties freak me out!" said the director.

My friend whipped off the tie with a dash of confidence, threw it behind him into a wastebasket, then walked over to shake the director's hand. That gesture was not particularly a Hollywood thing either. After an awkward beginning my friend impressed the director enough to get the job—or gig as they like to say. Next time he showed up in shorts and a T-shirt.

Another thing you might want to do is simply ask the person who is inviting you to interview what dress would be appropriate. They will normally be very willing to give you that information even if it is the CEO who will be interviewing you. The fact that you made the inquiry says something about your attention to detail and you will probably make an early impression they will remember.

What about online interviews over screen applications like Zoom? Don't make the mistake of wearing nice clothing on your upper body and nothing but underwear on your lower body. You may think you will never have to stand up but why not put some pants on just in case?

There is a famous story of a news anchor that did not normally do the Saturday broadcast. One weekend he was called in at the last minute to fill in for his buddy who suddenly became ill. He walked on the set and everyone scrambled to adjust their routine.

When the cameraman cut back from the weather report, the angle showed a side view of the anchor facing the weatherman. You guessed it. Not only was he wearing shorts, but he was sitting on a phone book.

Okay, maybe you're not going to anchor the evening news, but we've all heard stories of how embarrassing some moments can be when someone thinks the camera is off... and it isn't! And of course, that goes for phones and tablets as well.

On with the interview

If it is at a physical location, make sure you are several minutes early for your appointment. Not 30 minutes, but maybe 10. If you happen to arrive 30 minutes early, don't announce yourself; wait outside until you are just 10 minutes early. Some interviewers don't want to feel rushed by you being there too early. Whether you are too early or late, you are infringing on their valuable time. You don't want to be in a position of making excuses as your first impression.

The following information is totally applicable whether in a physical room or in an online chat room.

When you are invited into the office, make some small talk as soon as it is comfortable. Mention that you have been looking online and noticed that the company has just _____ (fill in the blank with something positive.) When they comment on your comment, show some sincere interest. Maybe the company is expanding and recently opened a new location in the area. By mentioning how impressed you are with the growth they are enjoying, you will establish some rapport. You get the picture.

You should go over your notes so many times that your research and preparation will just flow out of your mouth as though you had been talking about them for months. The conversation is easy and you are involved.

When you first meet with the individuals that will be conducting the interview, try mentioning something that you saw on their social media. Maybe you saw a picture of them bowling and let them know that you enjoy bowling as well. Ask them about their highest score (don't out do them). Talk about the aquarium that is in their office and how you had one when you were younger. Reflect on those notes that you took and come up with some very fluid and casual conversation that puts everyone at ease.

The Gibbs Interview

The next steps we are going to explore come from a presentation that I have enjoyed several times from Randy Gibbs. He is an extraordinary man with awesome skills in the interviewing process. His insights regarding interviewing include breakthrough concepts that make the entire process not only extremely productive but highly comfortable for everyone in the room. I use this information with his permission and feel honored to be able to put it in this treatise. I only hope to do it justice here. I will be using several of the slides from his slide stack.

The Crucial Keys to Highly Effective Interviews

The first thing that needs to be discussed is the mindset of an interview. It is very easy to enter an interview nervous and with trepidation. After all, you are going to sit in front of someone (or several someones) who may grill you to see how much you know and to see if they like your answers.

You have tried to prepare an answer for everything and especially the out of the box questions that have become the stuff of legend and folklore. Questions like, "How do M&Ms get their candy coating spread so evenly?" or "Why are manhole covers always round?"

Your hands are embarrassingly sweaty and your mind is racing, wondering, what will they ask me? How shall I answer them? What if they sense my anxiety and see the sweat beading on my forehead?

In reality, your mindset should be such that you are not the least bit nervous or concerned. You should have total confidence in what is about to happen. In fact, the interviewers should be the ones concerned. They should be wondering, by the end of the interview, how can we convince this person to come and work with us? What can we do to get them on board?

It is all in your mindset. Remember that the interview table or desk has two sides (or screens if you are online.) The parties on both sides are interviewing each other. Sure, the company is trying to see if you are worth hiring and will benefit their company, but you are also interviewing them to see if you want to work with them and if it will benefit you in your career plans.

You both have a job to do and the interview is where it all culminates. If you believe that you are in control, you are in control. As they say, that which you can believe, you can achieve. Our mindset is vital to our success.

So, what is the best way to prepare your mind for an interview? Approach it as a simple conversation, an open discussion and an opportunity of discovery.

Two Very Different Mindsets

Dependent

Inferior, dependent

Fear of failing, not getting the job

Anxious, nervous, stressful

Overly passive; sit and wait

Talk too much, listen too little

Press, try and convince them to hire me

Afraid to ask questions I.E., If I do, they might no like it (might not like me)

Collaborative

Peer to peer —Let's talk this over together

No such thing as failure

Engaging, curious, interested

Fosters confidence, comfortable with the process, clear

Eager to listen and learn from them what is most important

Striving for mutual gain, win/win

Courage to ask "hard" questions

Your mindset must change from feeling like the victim to believing you will be victorious. Make sure that what they see in you is confidence and someone who knows what they are looking for. Your positive thoughts will pass to them and they in turn will feel positive about the experience.

Remember, you are prepared with the conversation pieces, the introductions and the stories. You will direct the interview right into the path where you want it to be. You will be in the driver's seat right from the start.

Always strive for the collaborative mindset instead of the dependent. You are both there to achieve a goal and together you can do it!

The interview becomes a conversational roadmap

You want to go in a specific direction and frankly, whether they know how to steer or not, the interviewers actually want to travel down that same road. Sometimes, they don't know quite how to get there. Your approach will give them that direction and get things moving in the right direction right from the start. You both want the same thing, an open, comfortable, productive conversation.

We Both Want the Same Thing

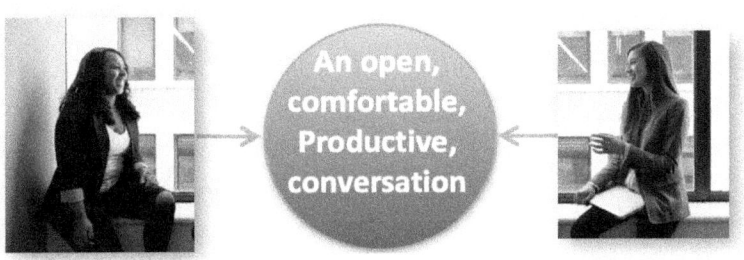

Think about them as a friend that you are going to talk to about the open position. Make it as conversational as you possibly can.

Most interviewers don't like the grilling method. They would like to have a cordial conversation that leads to everyone getting all the understanding they need in order to make the correct decisions.

If you have carefully reviewed the job description, you should have considered what resonates with you and your skills. You should have a feel for the parts of the job description that excite you and the ones that don't.

Think about the questions that entered your mind when you were going through the job description. You should feel free to ask those questions.

Exercising Your Influence in an Interview

When I interviewed job candidates, I never liked firing questions at them and making them feel uncomfortable or nervous. I always felt a level of tension in an interview and wasn't sure how to resolve it.

When a job seeker came prepared with thoughtful and relevant questions, it took a lot of the pressure and tension out of the interview for both of us. I was always impressed and relieved when the candidate took the initiative to steer the interview down a positive path.

– Brent Spurgeon – IT Executive

The steps of the productive interview

Pay close attention to the order of things and the natural progression of the experience.

You have done your research on the company and, if possible, the interviewers. You can make that comfortable contact and start a bit of a conversation to help them get conformable with you. Remember not to be too long because they have a limited time for your interview. Just break the ice and relax.

After you have broken the ice, immediately let them know that, although you are looking forward to answering their questions of you, you would like to start by asking them just a couple of quick questions. If you word it well, they will normally respond with "certainly" or "sure, go ahead."

JOB SEARCH

1. Set Up

RIGHT UP FRONT, WE ENGAGE IN A CONVERSATION
AWAY FROM THE TYPICAL ONE-SIDED INTERROGATION

"Than you very much for your time. I'm excited to learn more about your company and discuss your needs and my experience."

Make a Connection with the Interviewer

"When I was preparing for this interview, I noticed _____"
(Share something you found interesting.)

"As I've reviewed the description of this role, I see many areas where your needs and my experience match up well, AND I have a couple of questions. Would you mind if I asked you a quick question or two to get us started?"

Or you can say, "I know you have several questions of me and I'm happy to answer them. I also have a few questions. Would you mind if I asked a quick question or two to get us started?"

The slide shows several great examples of this transition. Practice how you will do it and become highly comfortable with your approach. It is vital that you get to ask the first questions! What are those questions? Before we go over the most important questions, it needs to be understood that we are asking because we are really vested in their answers. After you ask each of these questions, you need to drop everything from your mind and LISTEN carefully to their answers. Those answers will dictate the balance of the interview and make or break the outcome. Do not let anything else distract your mind from focusing on their answers.

This first key question is genius!

"What would you say are the one or two most important aspects of the role of this position?"

When you ask what the one or two most important aspects of the role of this position are, they will tell you exactly what they are looking for in a candidate for the position.

In a "normal interview" the interviewers ask a ton of questions to see if you have the skills to accomplish the most important aspects of the role they are trying to fill. They never tell you what those aspects are so you are left just answering their questions and being at the mercy of how they interpret your answers. By our asking that question, you now know exactly what they are looking for. There is no more relying on their interpretations. You can clearly define your abilities!

JOB SEARCH

2. Determine the Inteviewer's Priorities for this Role

"From your perspective as (name their title) what are the one or two most important aspects of this role that we should focus on today? I want to make sure we cover those areas."

If the answer is brief or vague, ask a follow-up question to clarify, such as:
"Would you min giving me an example of _____?"
or
"Can you please tell me a little more about _____ as it plays out in your company?"

If their answer is vague, follow up with a clarifying question.

"Would you mind giving me an example of_____?"

OR

"Can you please tell me a little more about _____ as it plays out in your company?"

Now you've had the interviewers clearly define the role and the position they are looking to hire. Next you want to understand what type of individual they think makes a good fit in that position.

This second key question is also genius!

"In your experience, what are some of the_____(key qualities, traits, attributes) of those who join your company that helps them to really thrive and add value and make them a good fit?"

Their answer to this question describes specifically what they are looking for in performance and what skills and traits they feel would make a candidate successful in the position!

JOB SEARCH

Culture, Values & Fit

THIS IS THE MAIN REASON COMPANIES INTERVIEW

"In your experience, what are some of the key qualities (or traits or attributes)
of those who join your company, really thrive
and add value, and are a good fit?"

Note: If their answer is vague or generic, ask a follow-up question to clarify.

Think about what you have just accomplished by asking these two genius questions. You have just uncovered exactly what they are looking for and the most important items on their agenda.

The answers to those key questions are exactly what they will be discussing when you have left the room. They will be thinking and talking about whether or not you are their answer to those exact questions.

Now they don't have to ask dozens of questions to find out if you have the skills or the personality traits to do the job. Because you already know exactly what they want, you will start telling them precisely how you will fit in and how your skills will benefit their company.

The interview hasn't even started and you know exactly what they are looking for! It is like having a cheat sheet handed to you just before the test begins!

Now it is your job to quickly recall and organize the personal stories that you have been memorizing. Your time spent preparing for general questions now leads you in a focused direction. You have more clarity on the items in the job description and you can easily align your strengths and focus all of your answers to demonstrate the qualities and skills that they have just told you that are looking for.

They are about to realize how fortunate they are in finding such a solid candidate!

3. The Heart of Traditional Interviews

TRANSITION: "THANK YOU.
NOW WHAT QUESTIONS DO YOU HAVE FOR ME?"

Power statements are crucial
Be concise, results-oriented and impactful
Employ the STAR method

Strive to align your answers with the:
• key priorities of the role
• qualities of people who "fit" well into the culture

As they ask you questions, make sure to "play catch" and keep it conversational.

• "Does that five you what you need?"
• "Did that answer your question?"
• "Anything else you'd like to discuss about this?"

Let's suppose that their answer to your first key question is that they are really looking for someone that is honest and has integrity because they will be dealing with sensitive information.

Let's say that their answer to your second key question is that they need someone who can be a team player but who can also step up and take charge if there is a need.

Then in your mind, you go through your STAR stories and you start putting them in order of experiences that show honesty, integrity. You prepare for sharing STAR stories of being both a good team member and also being a leader. You catalog those stories so that when they begin asking you questions, you can align all of your answers appropriately.

If they ask you about your most recent role in your previous employment, you will certainly tell them about that role while including a quick story that shows your adherence to the things they are looking for. A sample answer may be:

"I handled accounting for the advertising department and I was responsible for keeping close tabs on very sensitive information and only passing it on to the CEO."

Keep your answers fairly short and very focused and slanted to the desired traits.

When you have answered one of their questions, be sure to ask them something. Make sure they received all the information that they were seeking from the questions they asked.

You can say something like:

"Did that answer your question?"

Play catch and keep it conversational. Don't let the interview slide into the rut where they are firing questions and you are just giving answers. Make sure you are asking enough questions to keep it from being a grilling.

Active Listening

You may be familiar with this term. As opposed to just hearing someone, an active listener really understands what they are saying and can tune into their meaning and feelings.

When the interviewers say something, you need to nod your head and show genuine interest. At regular intervals you should repeat back something they said, or give some other acknowledgement that you understand them.

Author Stephen R. Covey said one of the habits of highly effective people was that they engaged in conversation with the goal of first understanding the other person. There is nothing wrong with starting a conversational response with, "So if I understand you correctly, what you are saying is…"

As mentioned before, the interview is normally set to a specific time limit so keep your eye on the clock. It is very important to make sure that they don't leave the conversation not knowing everything that they wanted to know.

4. Wrap-Up

WE INITIATE THE WRAP-UP
TO MAKE SURE BOTH OF US GET WHAT WE NEED

---

1. "What is the next step in the hiring process?" or "Where do we go from here?"

2. "What is your time frame for filling this role? When can I expect to hear back?"

3. "If I haven't heard back by then, would you mind if I followed up?"

When there are four or five minutes left, ask them the question:

"Before we run out of time, I want to make sure you have everything you need to make a good decision. Is there anything else you'd like to discuss?"

Make sure they get all that they need. Then, when they end it, be sure to thank them for their time.

Remember, they have been interviewing you, but you have also been interviewing them. You should have enough information to know if you want to go forward or not. If you know you want to go forward, you should make a positive statement that shows that you are very much interested in the position.

"Thank you so much for your time, and I want you to know that I am really interested in this position. I hope you will consider how I may be a good fit in your company."

Be sure to ask what the next steps are and what the timeframe is for filling the role.

"May I ask what the timeframe is for filling this position?"

When they answer, you should respond with a statement that shows you will be anticipating their communication.

"That sounds great. I look forward to hearing from you then. If for some reason there is a delay may I contact you?"

If they give you permission to contact them, be sure to do it.

Another typical part that comes at the end of an interview is for the interviewer to simply ask, "Do you have any other questions?"

Make sure you have saved at least one question for this moment. It demonstrates that you have been engaged in the entire interview and you are still interested even at the end. Make it a good question. Here's an example:

"You mentioned the new project. It sounds like something that could really be a growth opportunity for the company. Do you see me as a possible fit for that project and team?"

Whatever key point was mentioned during the interview, be ready with a final question that is substantial but not overwhelming.

Express Gratitude

If it feels right, send a text or email to the interviewers and thank them again for their time and express your continued interest in the position. Back in the day it was encouraged to actually mail a thank you card.

Let me take a moment to use this topic as an excuse to discuss another form of expressing gratitude. This comes from a mentor who had once experienced drug addiction, lost everything, and climbed all the way back to becoming a respected life coach. In one of his books he discusses the empowering effect of expressing gratitude to a higher power. While I myself choose to remain neutral in this job search book about whether or not one should pray to God for help in finding employment, I do think this story I'm about to share is an appropriate way to close.

The story is told of a man who had been unemployed for several months. He went to a job interview for an administrative position supervising employment counselors in his state. Being unemployed himself, he felt keenly aligned with this opportunity. He met with three people who he immediately respected and with whom he wanted to be associated.

After the interview, he took the elevator down to the lobby and felt the need to pour out his soul to God. He found a private place, sat down and rested his head in his hands. He gave thanks for being led to such an opportunity. In his words, "the experience was like a light started shining in my soul. I had a sense of well-being that I had not felt for a long time."

The man went home and told his wife that he had a really good feeling about getting the job.

Two days later his phone rang and he looked at the number. Was this finally going to be an answer to his prayers?

In less than 10 seconds he heard the words, "We've decided to go in a different direction."

Although devastated on the inside, the man found enough composure to say, "Well, thank you for letting me know."

But was the man truly thankful? He searched his feelings about the experience and bowed himself again in prayer. "Why?"

While in this state of mind he remembered that the feeling he had two days previous wasn't necessarily one of assurance that he would get the job, but more of approval for all he had done in making the effort to get the job. Instead of shaking his fist at heaven, he humbly gave thanks again for the opportunity and experience. And then he got that feeling again, "a comforting light shining in my soul."

My purpose in relating that story is that I personally learned something that I have found valuable for survival. Expressing gratitude, no matter how dark the situation, lifts us out of despair. We not only set a good example and spread a little positivity to others by doing so, I believe expressing gratitude ennobles us.

Oh, and you might be asking if the man ever did get a job, yes, he did. And now that I have included his story in my book, the job he *didn't* get has a message that can serve many of us. Maybe that was part of the higher purpose of his experience.

Interview Summary

1. Frame the interview as a conversation and not as an interrogation.

2. Determine the interviewer's priorities for the role.

3. Determine the most important aspects of the role and the most valuable traits of someone who would be a successful fit. Focus on them.

4. In the heart of the interview make opportunities to tell your STAR stories. Play a back and forth game of catch with your conversation.

5. Wrap it up by making sure that both of you got what you needed out of the interview.

This process for interviewing works astoundingly well. The results are tremendous. In all but one of the several interviews I had after learning this sequence, the interviewers said to me that our interviews were the best interviews they had ever had and that they enjoyed the time. I did nothing to request such a response. They really felt that way.

Conclusion

This treatise is simply designed to help you move through the job search process. I included tips and resources that I personally found most helpful, or in some cases, directed you toward information you need to get that next job for which you are well suited.

You may have noticed that I never used the term "dream job." While I do wish you the best of luck in finding your dream job, the reality is that most of us have to work because we need the money. I personally think it is better to prepare yourself to accept the fact that no job will check off ALL the boxes on the dream job chart. That said, I certainly have found job satisfaction most of my life.

I encourage you to be a realist. Don't set your expectations too high, but don't set them too low either. And if you accept a position that is less than you had hoped for, who's to say you can't strive to make it better?

Maybe a dream job is what you make it.

As I said at the beginning, what I have really presented here is a compilation of the best help I received from employment experts when I myself was looking for my next job. It took me

JOB SEARCH

nearly eleven months to learn this process. Hopefully you have now learned the same things – or what I would call the most important and helpful things – in just a matter of days.

This is not intended to be an all-encompassing resource for finding employment. There are literally thousands of resources on finding employment with at least as many suggestions and plans. Nevertheless, I sincerely believe the information you have here is very valuable. And I want to thank the amazing men at the employment center again. They touched me in a way that made me want to share them with others who may be working through that struggle of being unemployed or underemployed.

I know how difficult it is! I truly hope that this small resource is of some help to you in your search. Best of luck (and solid preparation) to you!

LYMAN ROSE

Special Thanks

Randy Gibbs
Doug Jeppson
Brent Spurgeon
Maikel Bailey
Rich Baron
David Stuart
William Hoeksel
David Mathis

Thank you for your patronage.
It would mean the world to us
and help others find employment
if you would take a moment and leave a review.

May you find other enriching titles available from Walkercrest

Please send any comments or suggestions to:
publishing@walkercrest.com